Knowledge Mapping

THE ESSENTIALS FOR SUCCESS

Wesley Vestal

APQC.
PUBLICATIONS

APQC
123 North Post Oak Lane, Third Floor
Houston, Texas 77024

Edited by Debra Beachy, Krystl Campos, and Rashi Mehra
Designed by Fred Bobovnyk Jr

Manufactured in the United States of America

ISBN 1-932546-48-0

APQC
Web site address: www.apqc.org

Contents

Preface v

Introduction: Why Map Knowledge?. 1

Chapter 1: Understand Knowledge in Organization 7

Chapter 2: What is a Knowledge Map? 25

Chapter 3: Getting Started 33

Chapter 4: Creating a Knowledge Map 51

Chapter 5: Helpful Tools for Creating a Knowledge Map. 61

Knowledge Management Glossary of Terms 67

Preface

Global economic growth is racing ahead. Markets are merging. Competition is increasing. Faced with less and less time to make key decisions, organizational leaders need knowledge at their fingertips.

This book will show senior and line managers how to tap the wealth of knowledge often hidden within an enterprise. It will help leaders who are meeting the challenge of retaining knowledge in a global economy as they manage a demographic bulge of soon-to-retire workers. More importantly, this book is for managers who lead by example and who successfully adopt new approaches to achieve their goals.

For those who seek to uncover crucial knowledge and processes needed for their organizations to succeed, this book offers a clear, concise approach. It guides managers through the process of mapping knowledge by providing distinct types of knowledge maps as well as tips on how to choose the right focus and scope of knowledge mapping. Additionally, it provides mini-case examples using real-world problems to show how to successfully apply the principles of knowledge mapping.

This book also details the process of successfully identifying and mapping knowledge, including: collecting, reviewing, validating, storing, and sharing knowledge and information.

The advice in this book is based on over seven years of work and research conducted by Wesley Vestal, APQC's KM Practice Leader.

An internationally recognized resource for process and performance improvement, APQC helps organizations adapt to rapidly changing environments, and to build new and better ways to work and to succeed in a competitive marketplace. APQC works with organizations to identify best practices; discover effective methods of improvement; broadly disseminate findings; and connect individuals with one another and with the knowledge, training, and tools they need to succeed. Founded in 1977, APQC serves organizations around the world in all sectors of business, education and government.

Wesley Vestal currently leads APQC's Knowledge Management practice area. He has extensive experience in helping organizations focus their knowledge mapping efforts to uncover hidden knowledge assets. The principles of knowledge mapping that Vestal has described in this book can be applied in many ways inside organizations of any size or sector.

Introduction

Why Map Knowledge?

Imagine planning your next vacation. What process do you use, either explicitly or implicitly, to actually arrive at your destination? Most people envision their "ideal state," which may be mountains, beach, relaxation, or adventure. Next, you grab a map to determine where this "ideal state" exists – for some, proximity is key, while for others, the more exotic the better. Then you research methods of getting there and where to stay once you arrive. Both require some knowledge of the area, which many of us find on the Internet, through friends, or from a travel agent. Finally, you "execute your process" by making reservations, buying tickets, getting in the car, and arriving for your week of fun. How does this relate to knowledge mapping? This scenario is remarkably similar to the typical business planning processes we use at work. In both vacation and business planning, a key ingredient in arriving at our destination is understanding how to get there – and maps are a great tool for making that easier and more efficient.

Business planning typically involves several steps of prioritization and the use of numerous tools. Senior managers frequently begin their business planning cycle by identifying several key goal areas for the near future. These may include increased productivity, lower costs, or deeper penetration into a key market. Input may come from customers, market research, new trends, or visionary thinking. Next, they typically create scenarios of what must occur to achieve these goals, such as increased resources, process improvement, new talent acquisition, or a merger. Then, business managers get involved in looking at how the processes they use will need to change or improve. Finally, employees execute those processes to achieve desired goals. How do employees and managers know where to go or how to get there? Knowledge-rich organizations map their internal and external knowledge resources to the goals, processes, and activities they feel will help them achieve success. Maps help inform managers and employees alike about areas of strength and weakness, as well as the connecting pathways that can make a trip easier.

However, knowledge mapping is not an end in and of itself. It is a tool, like a map, that helps you get from point A to point B more efficiently. It is a precursor activity to designing a knowledge management initiative.

MANAGING KNOWLEDGE: A CRITICAL TASK

If organizations do not fully leverage their existing expertise, then they risk losing a valuable asset: internal know-how. Organizations capture, transfer, and use knowledge in order to attain strategic goals in a more efficient and innovative manner.

Prior to 1995, few tools existed to understand what knowledge was embedded in organizations or analyze the flow of knowledge in organizations, and any methodologies for improving flow and use were miles away from materialization. In other words, knowledge management was a theory struggling to find application in reality. For more than a decade, APQC has worked on establishing methods and conducting benchmarking studies that have refined the practice of knowledge management.

Today, most large organizations have caught on to the importance of managing knowledge and have begun to embed explicit knowledge management activities into their operations. These activities connect people to people and to the knowledge and information they need to act effectively and to create new knowledge. Capturing lessons learned, reusing designs, transferring best practices, and enabling collaboration and access to expertise are a few of the approaches that organizations are adopting as part of their knowledge management initiatives. By opening up avenues for knowledge and information exchange, organizations can avoid repeating mistakes, save time locating standard information, and be better equipped to respond to changes in the marketplace. Using proper implementation, a knowledge management initiative can improve an organization's performance from the enterprise level to the bottom-line.

MAPPING KNOWLEDGE: THE CRITICAL FIRST STEP

Anyone undertaking a knowledge management initiative must first uncover what knowledge already resides in their organization. Like a traveler preparing for a road trip, business managers must be aware of two aspects of their journey: where they are headed and how they are going to get there. A map can provide a visual depiction of the terrain leading to a final destination, making the trip easier and the goal attainable. Similarly, a knowledge map highlights and organizes knowledge assets, so that managers and employees quickly understand gaps in knowledge, uncover key knowledge resources, and learn where to find in-house experts who can offer advice.

One of the fundamental tenets of knowledge management is that knowledge must link to and improve business processes. Without a map of the processes, goals, and knowledge assets inside one's organization, it will be difficult to reach one's destination. It is a key first step to a knowledge management initiative; however, just having a map will not actually get you to your final goal. You must still drive to your goals, operate your processes, and manage staff. Knowledge mapping is an active phrase because the act of mapping, of understanding and linking pieces of the organization together, is the important concept. Maps are wonderful resources but must be constantly updated to meet shifting needs and new challenges.

Knowledge mapping is quickly gaining favor across a wide spectrum of industries as a formidable tool for identifying knowledge, gaps in skills, and opportunities for improving organizational performance through knowledge sharing or reuse. In fact, large scale content management efforts in every industry depend on many of the basic tenets of knowledge mapping. APQC has worked with organizations in the oil and gas industry, nonprofit organizations, the military, and engineering firms to create mapping methods to improve business performance. We'll discuss how you can benefit from these lessons learned and improve your business processes by developing a clearer understanding of your knowledge landscape.

Knowledge maps can be used to:
- compile expertise locators that track internal and external resources,
- identify opportunities to reuse information,
- locate grassroots knowledge stewards,
- identify knowledge dependencies within cross-functional work groups,
- categorize value-added information resident within an organization,
- highlight key human, social, and structural knowledge,
- identify knowledge-sharing opportunities and barriers,
- develop bodies of knowledge for formal communities of practice, and
- create a knowledge tool that helps users find what they need.

This book is for any business or knowledge management practitioner who wishes to identify the embedded knowledge in their organization and the knowledge necessary for reaching a particular goal. It should be treated as a guidebook that will walk participants of a knowledge management initiative through the steps of creating a customized knowledge map—a visual depiction of critical knowledge assets that reside in his/her organization. Much like process mapping, effective knowledge mapping processes are best performed by people who intimately understand the business processes, knowledge assets, and expertise of the people in the organization, such as business process owners, talent management groups, and KM practitioners. Knowledge mapping concepts will be useful for knowledge management, talent management, succession planning, social network analysis, communities of practice, after action review/lesson learned exercises, and documentation/interview projects.

HOW TO USE THIS GUIDE

This guide begins with an explanation of the basic principles of knowledge. Next, it discusses: the role of knowledge in an organization, what a knowledge map is, how to get started by selecting the appropriate knowledge map, various applications of knowledge maps, and finally, some helpful tools for creating a map. In addition, this book outlines some of the most important critical success factors to consider in mapping an organization's knowledge.

In the initial chapters, readers can take advantage of a summarization of the guiding principles of mapping and managing knowledge. Chapter 3 includes an important survey to determine what type of map best fits a situation. An in-depth explanation of the steps involved in creating a knowledge map follows in Chapter 4. Chapter 5 details a number of sample applications of knowledge mapping, and finally, Chapter 6 closes by sharing some helpful tools and general insights into the knowledge mapping process.

The advice in this book is based on a decade of research on KM projects with more than 300 organizations. An internationally recognized resource for process and performance improvement, APQC helps organizations adapt to rapidly changing environments, build new and better ways to work, and succeed in a competitive marketplace. APQC works with organizations to identify best practices; discover effective methods of improvement; broadly disseminate findings; and connect individuals with one another and with the knowledge, training, and tools they need to succeed. Founded in 1977, APQC serves organizations around the world in all sectors of business, education, and government.

Like its membership base, APQC's work in knowledge management stretches across industries and around the globe. APQC's members are from various sectors, of various sizes, and most of them operate globally. APQC has researched knowledge management best practices in the defense, automotive, banking, energy, technology, consulting, education, health, manufacturing, pharmaceutical, retail, and telecommunications industries, as well as the government sector, to name just a few. This breakthrough learning occurs when organizations work outside their own industry and learn from others.

Just as builders survey the land before beginning construction, this guide should help you construct a map of what lies before you so that you can create a more efficient, higher quality organization that fully taps into its knowledge base.

Chapter One

Understand Knowledge in Organizations

KNOWLEDGE DEFINED

Before we begin with a discussion of knowledge mapping, it is appropriate to spend some time talking about knowledge and knowledge management as a frame for tools. At first glance, knowledge is easy to conceptualize. It is understood among knowledge management (KM) practitioners as a collection of information, experiences, and perceptions that is built upon as individuals carry out their lives. Forever a work in progress, knowledge evolves as people gain fresh perspectives from embracing new challenges, relationships, and situations. The knowledge an individual possesses can be a powerful tool in unleashing his/her potential for growth—in the personal or professional realm. But if someone were asked to categorize every piece of information that they knew, where would they began?

Now imagine an organization: A single environment where hundreds of people from diverse educational, cultural, and professional backgrounds share and use their knowledge in order to achieve strategic goals. Extending the concept of knowledge to organizations exponentially increases the complexity and value of the term. Often, in an organizational setting, *knowledge* is co-mingled with *information* and *data,* as if there were no distinction between the three. While it is important not to confuse these terms, all of them can be part of knowledge mapping efforts.

- *Data* can be facts and figures presented out of context. Although data can trigger innovation or improve efficiency, it lacks inherent meaning and provides no sustainable basis for action. It is a set of discrete and objective facts. There is no inherent meaning to data; data only describes what has happened. It provides no interpretation or judgment. There is no basis for action from data; too much data makes it hard to find and make sense of data[1].

- *Information* on the other hand, is data presented in context so people might make use of it. Information sources may include: patents, trademarks, processes, manuals, drawings, reports, research, transaction data, and market research. Data becomes information when its creator adds meaning. Information has relevance and purpose; information is a message. Information is meant to change the way the receiver perceives something and to have an impact on his/her judgment and behavior. Information is data that makes a difference[2].

- *Knowledge* is information put into action by people to accomplish an end goal (which may include gaining knowledge itself. This typically includes the rules and context of its use. Sources of knowledge can incorporate your customers, products, and processes; heuristics (or "rules of thumb"); skills and experiences; know-how; and pinpointing "how things work around here." Knowledge is broader, deeper, and richer than data or information. Knowledge exists within people; human beings transform information into knowledge. Knowledge develops over time through experience and includes what we absorb from courses, books, mentors and informal training. Too much knowledge can become "data" that people don't know how to use.

---

[1] Davenport and Prusak
[2] Ibid

KNOWLEDGE TYPES AND CONTEXTS

APQC and others have identified three general categories of knowledge: explicit, tacit, and implicit knowledge.

Explicit Knowledge

Explicit knowledge is also known as formal/codified knowledge. This type of knowledge resides in books and documents, formulas, project reports, contracts, process diagrams, lists of lessons learned, case studies, white papers, policy manuals, etc. Explicit knowledge is easier to document and share. It contributes to efficiency, and is easier to replicate. However, it may not be useful without the context provided by experience.

Tacit Knowledge

Tacit knowledge, also known as informal/uncodified knowledge, requires a little prodding to uncover. It includes know-how, past experiences, and expertise that can be found through interactions with employees and customers and through the memories of past vendors. This knowledge is hard to catalog, highly experiential, difficult to communicate and document in detail, ephemeral, and transitory. It is also the basis for judgment and informed action. Tacit knowledge leads to competency and a higher competitive advantage.

Implicit Knowledge

Implicit knowledge requires a bigger investment of time and energy. It refers to the middle ground of knowledge that has not been codified. It can be captured and written down once people explore the full depth of a vital process.

Organizational knowledge (whether explicit, tacit, or implicit) usually emerges from four contexts: cultural, historical, and functional.

1. **Social/Cultural knowledge** is collected from working in an organization's environment and developing the capacity

to collaborate with a variety of parties. It also entails the accumulation of standards of behavior, hierarchical relationships, and even things like dress codes that help employees "get things done" inside the confines of a particular culture.

2. **Historical knowledge** stems from the history of the organization, ranging from its creation to the present (including past business deals, legacy systems, relationships, and previous methods of management).

3. **Human knowledge** is the knowledge of personal individual capabilities and skills. While this knowledge can be buffed and improved through training, new roles, and coaching, an understanding of skills and weaknesses helps organizations develop better teams.

4. **Functional knowledge** is needed to operate the functions and processes to get the job done. This knowledge can be created or used when undertaking a technical operational process, during project management, or from general knowledge about a client's needs.

In order to facilitate easier map viewing, cartographers created universally accepted symbols to represent various features, including rivers, mile markers, bridges, and directions. Similarly, you should create a common set of symbols for your maps so that you can quickly label the various types of knowledge and content you find. These may include the following:

- People:

- Projects:

Workflows and Processes

- Best Practices/
  Lessons Learned:

- Position Papers/
  White Papers:

- Training/
  Learning Modules:

- Communities
  of Practice:

- Documents/Files:

These simple symbols and categories may help you create a map that is more functional and useful than simply dumping a long list of items into an Excel spreadsheet. For more information on tools for knowledge mapping, see Chapter 6.

Consider the following example: Company XYZ's marketing department needs to revamp a company brochure for an upcoming conference. The brochure should convey the image of the corporate culture and sell the company's products, using proven success strategies.

The group might draw from many sources while brainstorming ideas for the project. These sources could include the organization's history, cultural values, working environment and previous successful brochures. Additionally, the group could include specific functional knowledge, filtered through the experience of the group members. All of this will help ensure that the brochure meets with acceptance .

As this example demonstrates, knowledge is multidimensional. Explicit, tacit, and implicit knowledge can be extracted from either a cultural, historical, or functional context. Understanding this relationship will be extremely useful when designing a knowledge map as the crucial first step of your knowledge management initiative.

KNOWLEDGE MANAGEMENT: THE BIG PICTURE

All employees must incorporate knowledge management practices, both formal and informal, into their daily activities in order to improve their business operations and to help the organization maintain a competitive edge. More and more, organizations that make an effort to understand and harness their knowledge are seeing and reaping the benefits. In APQC's recent benchmarking report, *"Measuring the Impact of Knowledge Management,"* best practice organizations chronicled a 200 percent return on the investments they were making in knowledge sharing, including cost savings, productivity gains, quality improvements, and revenue gains[3].

---

[3] *Measuring the Imapct of Knowledge Management,* APQC 2004.

BASIC PRINCIPLES OF KNOWLEDGE MANAGEMENT

Knowledge management requires managers to work with complex and evolving issues, but there are some enduring principles of KM that are important to keep in mind as you use this book[4].

1. Knowledge management initiatives succeed when executives aim efforts at a clear set of value propositions, such as improving customer-related practices, reducing time-to-market, or achieving new levels of operational excellence. The choice depends on the "value levers" in a particular marketplace.

2. If you build it, they will not necessarily come. Technology applications do not, in themselves, create a need or demand to change behavior or share knowledge. Technology is indispensable to knowledge management in modern organizations, but the road to effective knowledge management is littered with abandoned knowledge management "solutions" that were really just applications. These vehicles quickly run out of gas, if they start at all. It is critical to select and implement technology as part of a larger, systematic knowledge management change initiative.

3. It is a misstatement to say that people hoard knowledge. What people hoard is their time and energy; they reserve it for high payoff activities. Most people want to share what they know; they want to learn from others and not repeat the mistakes of the past. However, there are barriers to sharing. These barriers are often structural: there is not enough time, the process is cumbersome, they do not know the source or the recipients and are not sure they can trust the information, and they know instinctively that tacit knowledge is richer than explicit knowledge. To ensure knowledge management is successful, work on these barriers, rather than on the psychological make-up of your employees.

---

[4] O'Dell, Carla, *The Executive's Role in Knowledge Management,* APQC 2004.
[4] www.orgnet.com/sna (retrieved March 2005).

4. Whenever possible, embed knowledge sharing; capture, and reuse it in the work itself and provide value to those who participate. Employees should experience greater professional development and an easier time getting their work done correctly. Rewards and recognition are important, but they will not take the place of creating knowledge-sharing systems that succeed and provide value.

5. The transfer of best practices and communities of practice is the most common—and most effective—strategy. Every organization APQC has studied in its 16 KM consortium benchmarking studies relied on transfer of internal best practices as a predominant KM strategy. It was not the only strategy, but it was the most popular and effective way companies chose to find out and share what they know.

6. Cultivating a knowledge-sharing culture is the result of a successful knowledge management strategy. Some organizations are fortunate enough to start with a culture conducive to sharing knowledge, based on a strong professional ethic, corporate pride, and well-honed skills in teaming. However, this is not a prerequisite. Those organizations that do not have these cultural attributes need two prerequisites for building the culture of sharing: leadership support and practice.

7. Successful KM efforts typically employ a "push-me/pull-you" approach. A combination of push and pull strategies tends to work best. Push approaches are characterized by a desire to capture knowledge in central repositories and then push it out to the organization. In contrast, pull approaches expect people to seek the knowledge they need when they need it. Neither seems to be enough by itself.

Four Types of Knowledge Management Approaches

Traditional knowledge-sharing activities fall into four different categories, as Figure 1 shows. The major difference among the categories lies in the degree to which they depend on explicit versus

Knowledge Management Approaches

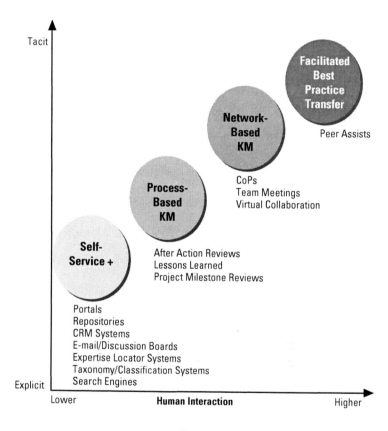

Figure 1

tacit knowledge and how much they involve human interaction versus technology.

1. **Self-service plus**—This approach engages the individual knowledge worker and is designed to increase his/her productivity by linking employees to information they need to do their job more effectively. Activities within this approach can

be accessed from the desktop or work site and include portals, intranets, and search tools. Content management systems also are used. They help employees identify, collect, categorize and refresh content by using a common taxonomy across the organization.

Self-service plus activities link people to whatever source of knowledge they need, be it other people, information about people, finding people with specific expertise, or knowledge for career development. Helping people quickly access instructions, data, and best practices helps to reduce cycle time, avoid relearning, and diminish hassles. The *plus* piece comes from the use of expertise location systems. This allows users to find expertise that can provide context for the subjects they are researching.

Knowledge mapping critical content, knowledge sources, and classification systems is a critical first step towards creating effective self-service tools.

2.   **Process-based KM**—Moving slightly away from explicit knowledge and depending more on human interaction, process-based knowledge sharing activities are designed to help employees and management capture, share, and reuse knowledge inside everyday work processes Activities that focus on the process include after-action reviews, lessons learned processes, and project milestone reviews. After-action reviews are learning/knowledge sharing processes that help organizations capture key lessons and identify improvement areas during and after important projects. Based on the U.S. Army's four question methodology, participants ask "What was supposed to happen?", "What actually happened?", "Why were there differences?", and "What did we learn?" Lessons learned is a knowledge-sharing process in which the participants debrief major events to capture lessons, best practices, and understand factors of success or failure. These also are known as "hot washes," "post-mortems," and "event debriefs." Project

milestone reviews typically are built in "gates" of the project management cycle and require teams to document and present outcomes for various stages of work. These should include any lessons learned that will help improve the next stage or benefit similar projects.

Knowledge mapping can help managers and team leaders identify the scope of after-action reviews as well as highlight the critical experts that need to be involved.

3. **Network-based KM**—This method integrates people as an important knowledge asset. Groups of people work together to create a shared space and shared objectives, either virtually or physically. Activities may include communities of practice (CoPs), virtual collaboration, and team meetings. Communities of practice are fast becoming the centerpiece for many organizations' KM strategies. These are networks of people that share information and knowledge in order to learn from one another. Usually, leaders, stewards and gatekeepers are formally appointed to capture best practices and steward a body of knowledge on behalf of the organization. Virtual collaboration is the joint effort of working together via a variety of technology tools (i.e. telephone, collaborative software, video conferencing, etc.) regardless of time differences and distance. Team meetings, while not traditionally lumped under knowledge management, are one of the oldest and most effective means of transferring knowledge within a specific group of people. The goal for network-based KM is to connect people together around specific business issues to help transfer tacit/un-codified knowledge.

Knowledge mapping helps to identify the scope, knowledge assets of the group, gaps in content, and sources of expertise that can help the group perform more quickly and with higher satisfaction.

4. **Facilitated Transfer of Best Practices**—This approach to managing knowledge has a huge return but also requires a significant investment. It uses structured processes to identify proven practices, capture the tacit and explicit knowledge within that process, deliver it to a recipient with a need, and measure the business impact of reusing that knowledge. This approach can be used in conjunction with other activities, such as CoPs, where tips and answers can be shared.

   Facilitated best practice transfer helps to quickly close gaps in performance or disseminate new practices and raise performance or create new benchmarks. Just because somebody tells you how to do something does not mean that you learned how to do it. You still have to put resources into changing your processes and your practices.

   Knowledge mapping is a vital component of transfer – it is crucial to understand what explicit content and tacit expertise one group has before it is possible to transfer to another. The recipient group also should knowledge map their practices to understand the gaps that need to be filled.

   Considering the basic principles and traditional approaches surrounding KM, it is clear that implementing a proper effort involves a lot of work. Keep in mind that the benefits: increased employee and asset productivity, facilitated learning, better and faster decisions, innovative product development, and improved customer relations, make the endeavor well worth the effort.

   Figure 2 offers a quick checklist of ways that you can create knowledge maps to assist with the creation or implementation of the four types of KM approaches listed above.

Implementing a Knowledge Management Activity or Initiative

   By focusing on a specific business need (targeting a value proposition), organizations can frame an approach and begin to

Quick Checklist on Knowledge Map Creation

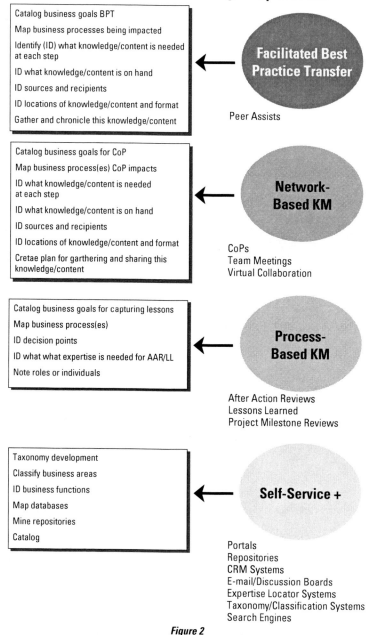

Catalog business goals BPT

Map business processes being impacted

Identify (ID) what knowledge/content is needed at each step

ID what knowledge/content is on hand

ID sources and recipients

ID locations of knowledge/content and format

Gather and chronicle this knowledge/content

Facilitated Best Practice Transfer

Peer Assists

Catalog business goals for CoP

Map business process(es) CoP impacts

ID what knowledge/content is needed at each step

ID what knowledge/content is on hand

ID sources and recipients

ID locations of knowledge/content and format

Cretae plan for garthering and sharing this knowledge/content

Network-Based KM

CoPs
Team Meetings
Virtual Collaboration

Catalog business goals for capturing lessons

Map business process(es)

ID decision points

ID what what expertise is needed for AAR/LL

Note roles or individuals

Process-Based KM

After Action Reviews
Lessons Learned
Project Milestone Reviews

Taxonomy development

Classify business areas

ID business functions

Map databases

Mine repositories

Catalog

Self-Service +

Portals
Repositories
CRM Systems
E-mail/Discussion Boards
Expertise Locator Systems
Taxonomy/Classification Systems
Search Engines

Figure 2

implement the stages of knowledge management. Regardless of the approach, APQC has defined a standard set of steps to follow.

The Road Map to Knowledge Management Results: Stages of Implementation[TM] is depicted in Figure 3.

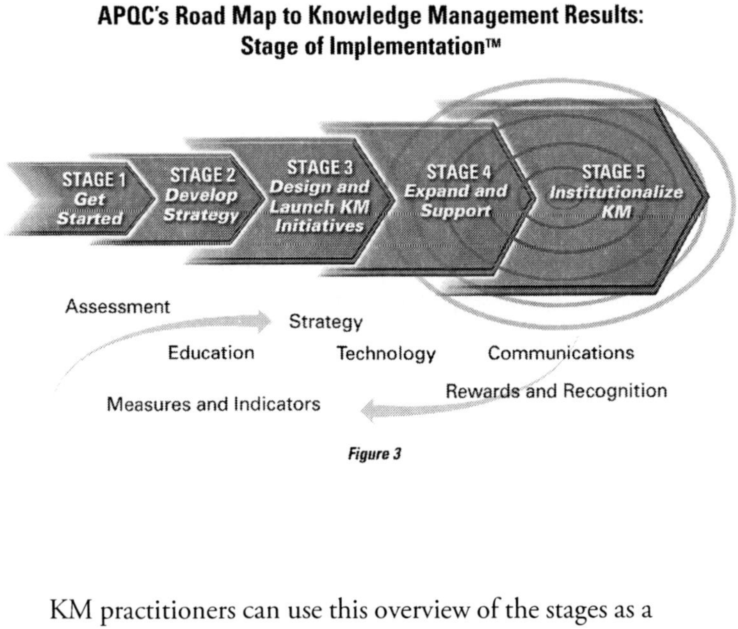

APQC's Road Map to Knowledge Management Results: Stage of Implementation™

STAGE 1
Get
Started

STAGE 2
Develop
Strategy

STAGE 3
Design and
Launch KM
Initiatives

STAGE 4
Expand and
Support

STAGE 5
Institutionalize
KM

Assessment

Strategy

Education   Technology   Communications

Measures and Indicators   Rewards and Recognition

Figure 3

KM practitioners can use this overview of the stages as a road map to understand where their organizations are in the KM journey, to see how others have successfully faced similar challenges, and to learn what might be done to move forward. Understanding the issues, seeing the signposts of problems and opportunities, and knowing the tools and tactics of others can help at any stage. Learning from others provides the opportunity to make new mistakes, not repeat those of others.

Each stage is described below as if it were distinct from the others. In reality, the stages flow into each other, as different parts of the organization move at different speeds and various elements fall into place. Some organizations move through the stages very quickly by learning from early adopters and barely stopping to notice they have moved to a new level of implementation. Stage 2 is the point at which most organizations spend time looking for the best way to improve business performance through more efficient knowledge sharing and reuse. Stages 3 to 5 is when the action tends to happen – from creating and launching initiatives to expanding and institutionalizing processes. There stages are about driving results. Knowledge mapping tends to happen most frequently in Stages 2 and 3, although it is a great tool to use no matter the maturity of the effort.

For more information on APQC's *Road Map to Knowledge Management Results: Stages of Implementation*[TM], check out APQCs *Passport Series* book of the same name.

The Four Cornerstones of Managing Knowledge

Knowledge management depends on the interplay of four key components. Engaging these four assets will enable an organization to move through each stage of an initiative in the most thorough and efficient way possible. Likewise, all four must be considered in a knowledge mapping effort. As Figure 4 (page 22) illustrates, there is an interdependence that exists among technology, people, and processes. Content here describes all three. Knowledge mapping, as we will discuss, can and should include the landmarks noted. The knowledge flow process in the middle denotes the typical process of knowledge creation, sharing, and reuse. The surrounding components of people, process, content, and technology describe the fundamental aspects of KM programs. Effective knowledge maps can explicitly depict the core and contextual knowledge that exists, regardless of source or form. When done properly, knowledge maps should help you move from point A to point B with maximum aplomb and minimum disruption.

1. **People**—People add the most dimensions to the process of knowledge management. Perceptions, experience, and personal

Knowledge Management

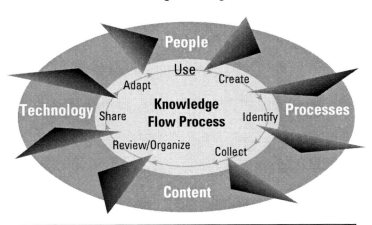

- People (Leadership, KM roles, SMEs, recognition, etc.)
- Processes (Shared standards, metrics, cross-organizational integration, feedback loops)
- Content (Explicit content, content management, taxonomies, validation, etc.)
- Technology (Portals, expertise location, repositories, search)

Figure 4

interpretations simply cannot be conveyed on paper as well as through verbal communication. Through training and communication, forming communities of practice (CoPs), designating knowledge managers, and creating a culture where employees share knowledge, people make it possible to harness knowledge and use it towards the organization's best interest. People embody expertise, competencies, cultural know-how, and specific roles, all of which are critical landmarks to capture and understand.

2. **Process**—Instituting processes to promote knowledge management is essential to maintaining a continuous flow of information throughout an organization. Processes designed to encourage collaboration, generate feedback, share standards, and engage metrics and reporting are technical but necessary to

implement knowledge management practices. Likewise, linking knowledge to business processes will help make sense of the workflow of the organization, helping business leaders translate maps into action.

3. **Content**— The discussion of content is often where knowledge mapping comes into play. Content arises from the overlap of the first three components. People gather content in order to make decisions, to complete their work, or to fulfill a process. Information and knowledge can be extracted from artifacts, best practices, standard operating procedure documents, books, training classes, learning modules, expertise, and advice.

4. **Technology**—Software programs are convenient tools to track and build upon knowledge that surrounds certain business processes. Expertise databases, file sharing, project management software, repositories and portals are accessible systems that compound knowledge sharing and promote knowledge management.

Chapter Two

What Is a Knowledge Map?

Much like the explorer described earlier who follows a travel map in the wilderness, organizations use knowledge maps to locate key internal knowledge and experts who can point the way. A knowledge map acts as a "snapshot in time" to help organizations understand what knowledge they have and where weak links exist. It also reveals what individual knowledge or expertise is critical to a process or focus area. Just like the road map in your car, however, maps quickly become dated as your organization changes, new employees replace older experts, and new goals emerge. Throughout this book, you will hear about knowledge mapping as a dynamic activity, not as a static collection of dusty knowledge maps. The process of linking your business goals and strategies together with your knowledge assets is where the power of this tool lies.

Knowledge mapping should start with the business of the business. What are the critical business goals or capabilities that senior management or customers focus on in the upcoming business cycle? What are the strategies that management is employing to meet those goals or capabilities? What processes link to those goals? Finally, what knowledge assets (either people, expertise, or content) do you have to make those processes work as efficiently as possible? Where are the gaps in your knowledge that might prevent those processes from making the necessary impact? How does the knowledge landscape help inform business managers about what needs to be added, changed, or improved?

Figure 5 is an example of a knowledge map. The top row of the map depicts the business process steps that employees typically engage in when attempting to sell a product inside a retail establishment. The left column represents the functions and regions that have an impact on that process. Inside the cells of the map, we have highlighted some of the information that you might want to capture in a map. This particular version, the "Expertise Tacit" map, will be described later in greater detail. In essence, this organization wished to identify what expertise was needed inside of the decorator services business function. Organizations can use this map to identify key experts or roles that can be interviewed for best practices, participate in after-action reviews, or provide insight about tasks within the process.

THE KNOWLEDGE FLOW PROCESS

Once you've uncovered the strategic goals, strategies, and processes that drive your business, it is important to consider how knowledge typically flows through the organization. This knowledge flow process, depicted in Figure 6 (page 28), outlines a conventional continuous cycle of knowledge creation and use.

Starting in the upper right of Figure 6 (page 28):
- **Create**—The creation of knowledge and information happens everyday in many different ways – new experiments, creative implementation plans for new clients, or tweaks to a standard operating process.
- **Identify**—Uncovering or highlighting new or existing knowledge or information is a critical step in the knowledge management chain. This may happen accidentally, as part of a knowledge audit, or in a brown bag luncheon.
- **Collect**—The process of collecting, capturing, and storing knowledge or information in a medium.
- **Review**—Validation or evaluation of knowledge or information for relevance, accuracy, and use.
- **Share**—The act of pushing knowledge or information to others. This may happen by storing assets in a database or standard

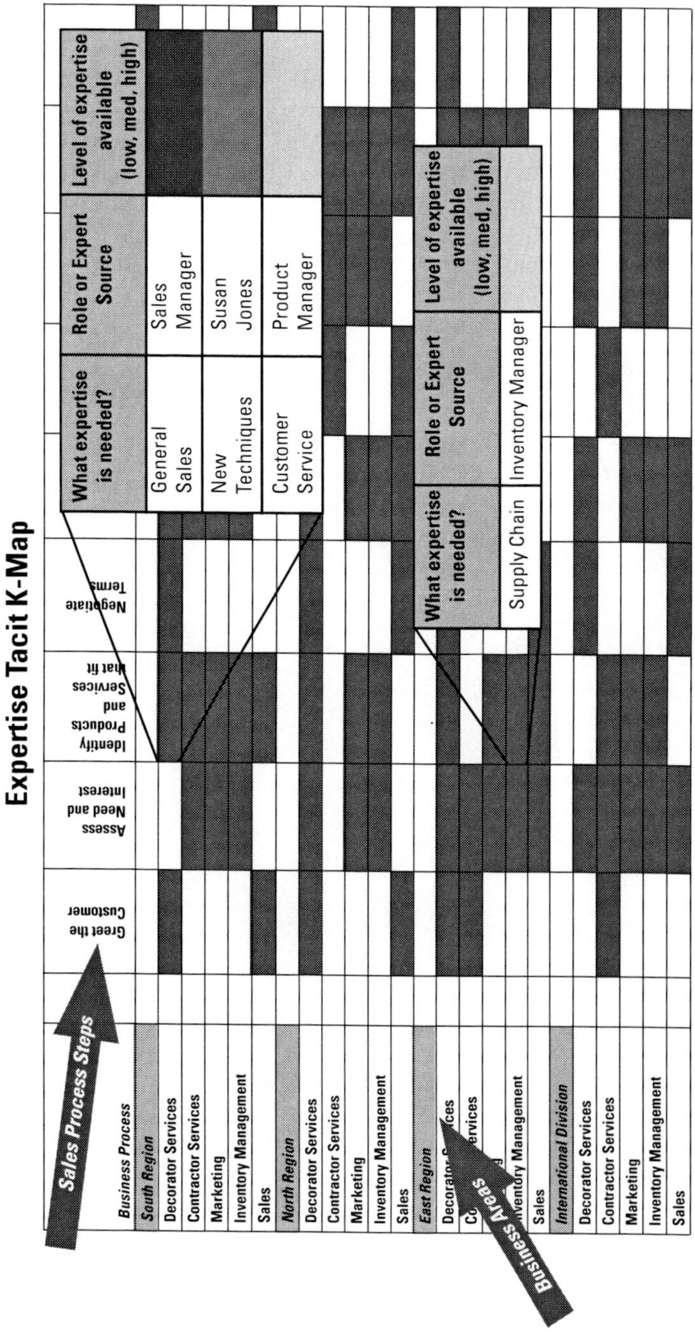

Figure 5

These are the people that should be included in the AAR process.

Knowledge Management

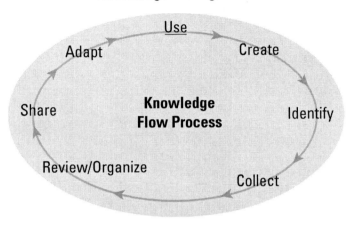

Figure 6

format, or by sending an email, hosting a presentation, or talking in the hallway.

- **Adapt**—The process of altering knowledge or information one receives or learns to fit local and current conditions.
- **Use**—The most important step in the process of managing knowledge – reusing the information or knowledge to improve outcomes, processes, and/or activities.

KNOWLEDGE MAPPING AND PROCESS MAPPING

Teams begin mapping their knowledge by identifying the core processes that need improvement. Process mapping is a wonderful precedent activity for knowledge mapping because it ensures that knowledge links to the ways people work. As we will discuss, it is not absolutely necessary to map a process when creating a knowledge map, but doing so will help ensure that you are focusing on improving business processes as well as provide a classification system for the knowledge and information you are mapping. A knowledge map can explicitly denote the knowledge needed for successful business process completion, as well as the gaps in knowledge and connections needed to improve. By connecting each phase of a business process to the current knowledge available, a knowledge management practitioner can create a map that traces where knowledge "lives," and make plans for improving it. Using APQC's Process Classification Framework (found at www.apqc.org) can help to illustrate the various areas where knowledge mapping can make a significant difference in business performance.

Why do you process map?
- Ensures that everyone understands the shared vision of a process
- Provides an accurate snap-shot of the process
- Aids in identifying non-value added tasks
- Facilitates training of new employees
- Assists in determining where in-process measures need to be used

How do you process map? There are dozens of texts, courses, and models for process mapping that one can probably find inside your own organization or on the Internet. Figure 7 (page 30) depicts an example of a fairly standard cross-functional process map. The steps to create a process map follow.

Step 1: Identify a small team that has deep knowledge of the process to be mapped; include as many functional areas as needed.

Step 2: Label the functions that engage in the process you are mapping, starting with the customer in the boxes along the left side (for a sales process this may involve sales, sales support, marketing, and regulatory).

Step 3: Identify the steps within the process and place these in the correct lanes on the map (steps may include identify target customer, assess need, and enter order into system).

Step 4: Sequence the steps until all within the group are satisfied that the process is adequately mapped; and

Step 5: Draw all connection lines between the steps.

Process Map Example

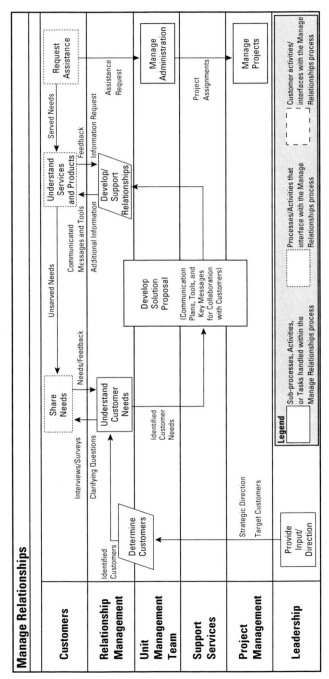

Figure 7

Use the following shapes in Figure 8 to create your process map.

Standard Process Mapping Shapes

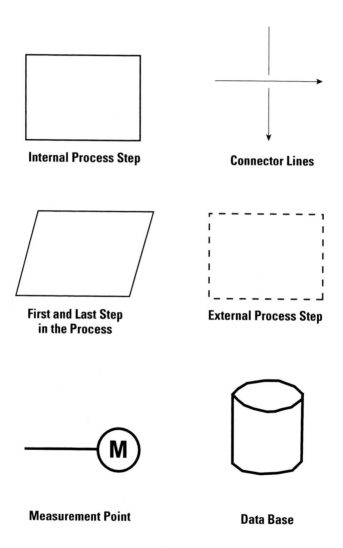

Figure 8

Consistent Factors for Success in Process Mapping
- Communication is key. It should take no more than a single sheet of letter size paper to communicate the activities in a process.
- Use a single level of detail only. Don't try to fit every possibility onto the map or flowchart. If you need more detail, add another level of map.
- Have a verb-noun agreement. Maps and flowcharts show action and so should processes and activities
- Label inputs and outputs. These are nouns. Key considerations—no outputs=no value.
- Post-it-notes and pencils. Using large format paper with these reduces the frustration level for the inevitable changes.

Linking Process Maps to Knowledge Mapping:

Today, processes represent the language of most businesses. In order to simplify the building of a classification system for knowledge, many practitioners agree that knowledge maps should be applied as overlays to process maps. This indicates knowledge flow and gaps in knowledge. As we will discuss later, knowledge mapping does not always have to relate to a specific business process; instead, it may be used to link knowledge to strategic goals, competencies or expertise areas, or job functions. However, a clear understanding of the business processes that drive those goals, competencies, or jobs, is critical to creating a map that allows you to take action. At its core, the knowledge mapping team should look at each process step and ask what knowledge is needed to successfully complete that step, what knowledge exists, and where that knowledge can be accessed. Other questions about the sources, recipients, format, and best delivery vehicles for that knowledge help to flesh out the details that make the map more useful.

Chapter Three

Getting Started

WHO SHOULD PARTICIPATE IN KNOWLEDGE MAPPING?

Once a process has been identified, a "knowledge" manager must identify the right people to participate in the process of knowledge mapping. Ideally, the most knowledgeable people about the process should be key players in creating the knowledge map. This list of players does not have to necessarily include managers, but it should recruit people who are significant owners of the process and who have a stake in that particular process. The group should be cross-functional in nature so that all areas of the business that supply input, operate the process, or receive output of the process have a chance to add their input. Additionally, the group must have some ownership over the findings of the knowledge map and be able to influence needed changes. Finally, having a neutral facilitator who can pull the disparate groups without getting bogged down by a particular agenda will help to smooth the process.

WHAT TYPE OF KNOWLEDGE MAP IS APPROPRIATE?

Knowledge maps correspond to a particular business process or goal. Just like a driver must know his destination before he looks at a road map, organizations must set a particular goal and trace the required knowledge for that process to have value. The key to getting started is determining what kind of outcome you are driving to. Do you need to understand what competencies or expertise exists inside the organization to meet specific business goals? Are you trying to create an after-action review process for a variety of functions to improve project schedule estimating? Are you creating a community of practice to increase collaboration and innovation opportunities? Or are you trying to determine where your organization is vulnerable to knowledge loss from retirement or downsizing? For differing applications, different maps are appropriate.

This section presents seven templates a knowledge manager can use in combination or individually as necessary.

A knowledge manager may only need one template for his/her current purposes, but it is quite likely that he/she will reapply and integrate other templates as the organization's needs evolve. All are based on similar constructs and questions – the differences lie in the questions one asks and in the outcomes one derives. Start with this simple assessment to help you determine what type of map and questions are most appropriate.

ASSESSING YOUR KNOWLEDGE MAPPING NEEDS

Knowledge managers can use this checklist to determine in the next section what type of knowledge map would be appropriate.

What is the most important thing for you to identify with a knowledge map?

A. knowledge needs for specific strategic business goals.
B. overall levels of expertise or knowledge.
C. gaps in knowledge or communication among units or groups.
D. specific expertise within a business unit or process area.
E. areas of the organization that need lessons learned or after-action review processes.
F. specific knowledge or content for a community of practice.
G. specific knowledge or content for a transfer of best practice initiative.
H. other: _____

_____

> Based on what a reader has checked in the preceding knowledge assessment, a specific map will be appropriate.
> - If you selected checkbox A, use the strategic overview knowledge map.
> - If you selected checkbox B or C, use the expertise overview knowledge map AND/OR the competency/learning knowledge map.
> - If you selected checkbox D or E, use the technical/functional knowledge map AND/OR the expertise tacit knowledge map.
> - If you selected checkbox F or G, use the document explicit knowledge map AND/OR the job/role-based knowledge map.

Identifying Barriers

The first barrier for knowledge mapping is a lack of understanding of the knowledge flow process inside your organization. Do functions and business units work independently? Are people who create knowledge able to easily collect and store that knowledge, or do they tend to hoard it? Do you have commonly accepted and widely used validation processes for maintaining the validity of expertise or content? Do people tend to distrust knowledge created by others or embrace it? Without a clear sense of all of the knowledge flow components, knowledge mapping is tough because you may miss out on important steps.

Another barrier is not having the right team members on a knowledge mapping team – the players must understand the business processes, strategic business goals, and have a good sense of what knowledge assets are needed.

A third barrier is the classic "knowledge is power" syndrome that exists in many organizations today (especially engineering and science-based organizations). In this case, employees are reluctant to share their knowledge with the rest of the organization because they feel threatened that sharing might lessen their importance as an employee.

A fourth common hurdle is the failure to understand what the business process looks like. Often, this involves not having a plan to collect, validate, store and reuse the knowledge and information about that business process once it is collected. Knowledge has a shelf life and requires constant updating and validating. Creating a map for the sake of doing so is not worth the time or effort; instead the team needs to map so that it can create more efficient processes, improve access to intellectual capital, and ultimately improve performance for the customer.

All of these hurdles can be overcome by training people on how to knowledge map, when to use various tools, and how to use knowledge maps to create solutions. Process improvement practitioners, found inside many organizations today, have many of the skills needed to successfully knowledge map. However, business managers and knowledge managers need to use these maps to effect change; after all, very few of us collect maps to then stick them on our shelves. Maps are tools that help us accomplish tasks more efficiently, so providing the skills and expertise to create them and use them is critical for success.

We have identified three main categories of knowledge maps, with seven different types of maps illustrated below. In our experience, different organizations have implemented knowledge maps in a variety of ways; however, most fit into one of these basic categories. We caution the reader that there is no exact or perfect map for all situations; instead, we have found that having a "buffet" of choices helps one pick and choose the aspects of the maps that fit. You will probably develop tweaks and nuances that fit your situation more closely than any text can offer, so have fun and be creative.

The categories are:

- **Enterprise Knowledge Maps**
  - Strategic Overview Knowledge Map
  - Expertise Overview Knowledge Map
- **Cross-Functional Knowledge Maps**
  - Expertise Tacit Knowledge Map
  - Technical/Functional Knowledge Maps
- **Process Explicit Knowledge Maps**
  - Document Explicit Knowledge Map
  - Job/Role-based Knowledge Map
  - Competency/Learning Needs Map

1. **The Strategic Overview Knowledge Map**—This type of map is large in scope and is used for achieving specific strategic goals. Use this map to identify and gauge the level of competency or expertise you have to meet the strategic business goals of the organization. The gap analysis is critical – once you've identified what you think is important, you should be able to create a plan of attack for closing gaps. How?
   - Develop or use existing business strategic goals.
   - Interview appropriate business management to gauge overall knowledge needs within the various areas of the organization to meet those goals.
   - Identify the following:
     a. Knowledge/competencies you need to meet each goal area
     b. Knowledge/competencies you currently have to meet each goal area
     c. Rate the gap between what is needed and what is available (red, yellow, green)
     d. Means to access the knowledge/competencies on hand
   - Use this map (Figure 9, page 38)) to identify areas where significant strategic knowledge gaps and strengths lie. The team can then determine whether to buy, build, or leverage knowledge to fill gaps.

Strategic Overview Knowledge Map Template

Strategic Business Focus Area	What knowledge and/or competencies are needed to achieve this strategic focus?	Priority of knowledge (1-5)	What knowledge and/or competencies do we currently have for this focus area?	Gap in knowledge	How is what we have currently accessible?
Identifying customers	Market Research Prospecting Alliances	5 3 2	Market Research		Intranet sites Shared drive CoPs
Sell work	Proposal writing Sales overview	5 2	Proposal templates		
Developing innovative solutions					
Customer service					

Big gap—a priority　　Some gap—develop plan　　No gap

Figure 9

2. **The Expertise Overview Knowledge Map**— Many organizations
    face a looming knowledge retention crisis with the aging of
    the baby-boomer generation. Industries such as oil and gas,
    manufacturing and the government can all expect to lose a
    majority of their current workforce due to retirement within ten
    years. This map is designed to provide a broad understanding
    of what knowledge the organization has in various parts of the
    business as well as identify its risk for disappearing. It identifies
    strengths and opportunities in expertise, knowledge, or sharing
    behaviors, as well as key assets that need to be available to other
    parts of the organization. The expertise overview map should be
    used in conjunction with succession planning maps from HR
    to help identify risk areas, plan for mitigation, and inform on
    development plans for current employees. How?

    - Identify the key areas and processes in your enterprise that
      need to be mapped.
    - Develop or use existing process maps to begin knowledge
      mapping.
    - Identify appropriate HR or personnel management to assist
      you with identifying expertise.
    - Interview appropriate business management to gauge
      overall levels of expertise within the various processes.
    - Assign colors to represent little or no expertise (red),
      mediocre expertise levels (yellow), or appropriate expertise
      (green).
    - Rate the risk of losing the current expertise due to
      retirement, skill gap, or turnover.
    - Identify the key roles or people that embody the expertise
      critical for your success.
    - Use this map (Figure 10, page 40) to identify hiring,
      training, or development needs. It also can identify major
      holes in knowledge flow.

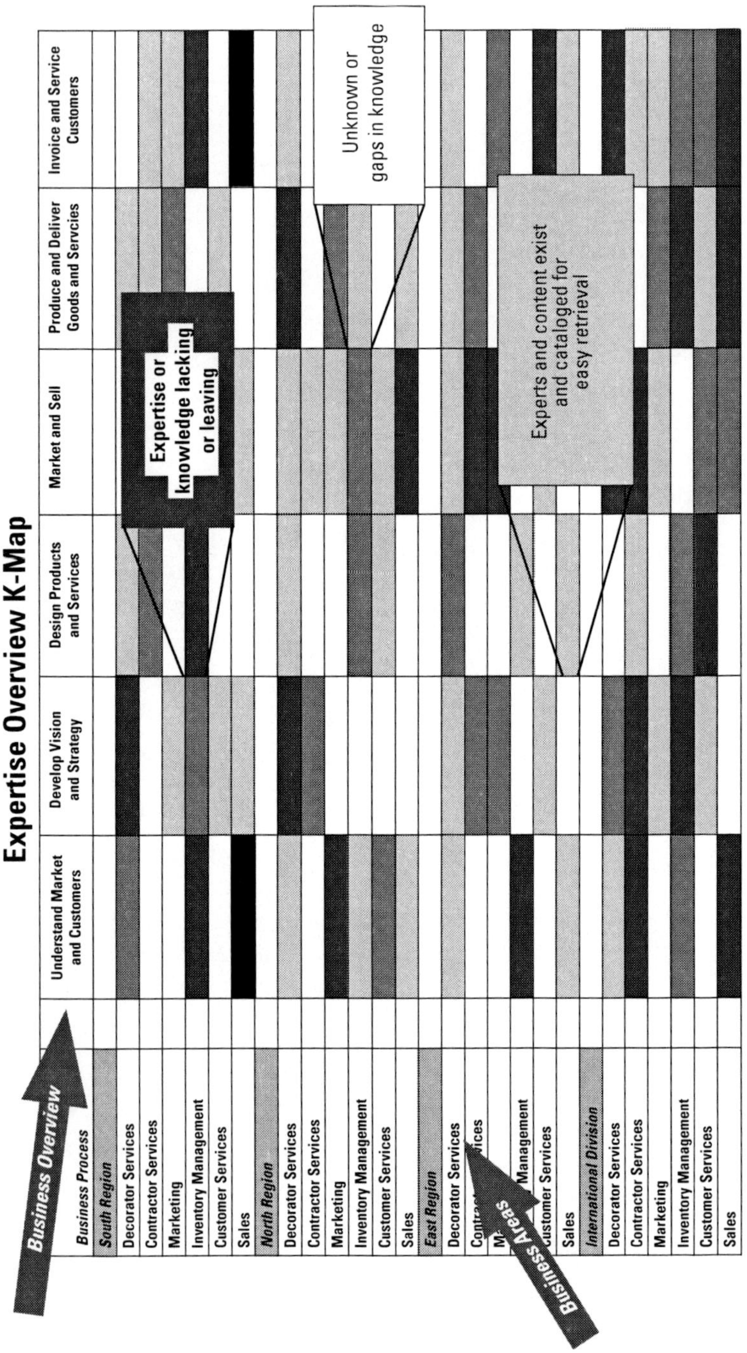

Expertise Overview K-Map

Business Process	Understand Market and Customers	Develop Vision and Strategy	Design Products and Services	Market and Sell	Produce and Deliver Goods and Servcies	Invoice and Service Customers
South Region						
Decorator Services						
Contractor Services						
Marketing						
Inventory Management						
Customer Services						
Sales						
North Region						
Decorator Services						
Contractor Services						
Marketing						
Inventory Management						
Customer Services						
Sales						
East Region						
Decorator Services						
Contractor Services						
Marketing						
Customer Services						
Sales						
International Division						
Decorator Services						
Contractor Services						
Marketing						
Inventory Management						
Customer Services						
Sales						

Business Overview

Business Areas

Expertise or knowledge lacking or leaving

Unknown or gaps in knowledge

Experts and content exist and cataloged for easy retrieval

Figure 10

3. **The Competency and Learning Needs Knowledge Map**—Unlike the expertise overview knowledge map, this type of map looks more explicitly at learning or competency needs within various business processes. If the previous map helps ascertain current assets and risks of losing those assets, this map helps your organization look forward at the capabilities it needs to meet its strategic goals. Specifying the learning needs associated with those goals can help you create a learning and development program that focuses on the business of the business. This is a common tool in use in sophisticated learning and development organizations today. How?

    –   Develop or use existing competency/learning areas to begin knowledge mapping (list across top)
    –   Identify appropriate HR or organizational learning development to assist you with identifying competencies.
    –   Then, interview appropriate business management to gauge what types of competencies/learning opportunities will help them drive business results.
    –   Next, identify the following:
        a. What knowledge is needed to fulfill this competency?
        b. What knowledge/learning can we deliver to fill this competency today?
        c. What is the ideal vehicle for delivering this knowledge/learning?
    –   Use this map (Figure 11, page 42) to identify hiring, training, or development needs. It also can help you uncover major holes in your current competencies or learning plans.

4. **The Technical/Functional Knowledge Maps**—The technical/functional knowledge maps can help your organization more clearly understand its strengths and gaps within specific technical or functional knowledge domains (e.g., ship design, component assembly, etc.). This map, in conjunction with the learning/competency maps, can be helpful tools for senior managers who need a snapshot of the expertise in critical technical disciplines or key business competency

Competency/Learning Needs Knowledge Map

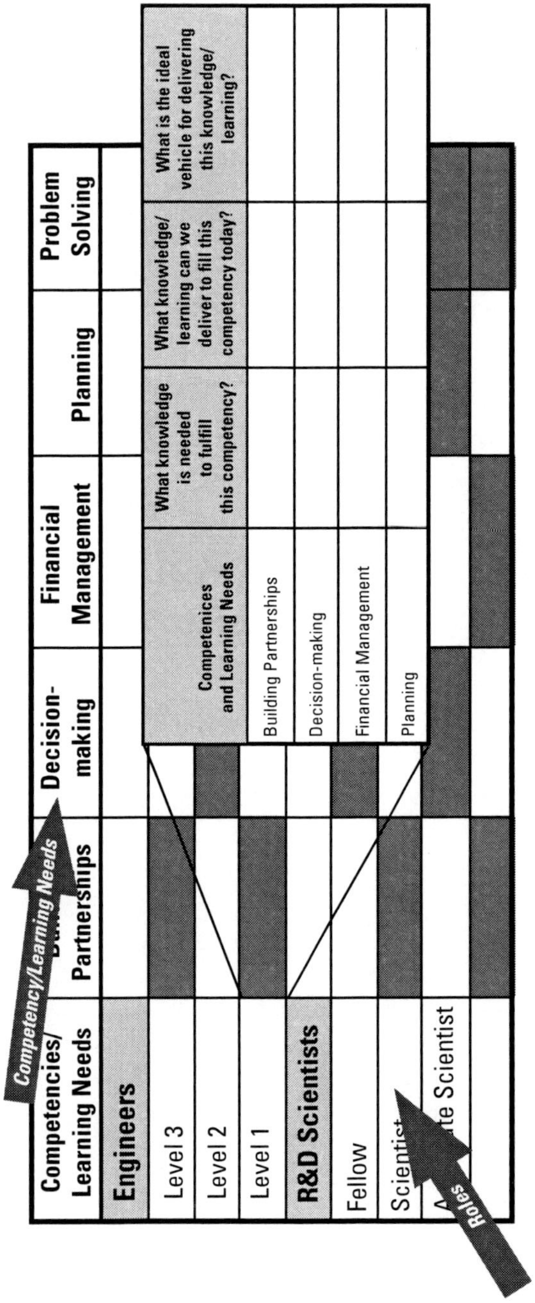

Competencies/ Learning Needs	Building Partnerships	Decision-making	Financial Management	Planning	Problem Solving	What is the ideal vehicle for delivering this knowledge/ learning?
			What knowledge is needed to fulfill this competency?	What knowledge/ learning can we deliver to fill this competency today?		
			Competenices and Learning Needs			
Engineers						
Level 3			Building Partnerships			
Level 2			Decision-making			
Level 1			Financial Management			
R&D Scientists			Planning			
Fellow						
Scientist						
...te Scientist						

Roles

Competency/Learning Needs

Figure 11

areas. The team can then perform a gap analysis to determine where opportunities for improvement lie and then create implementation plan to help them achieve their goals. How?

– Develop or use technical/functional knowledge requirements for specific jobs to begin knowledge mapping.
– Identify appropriate business management and experts to help you identify sources and owners of content/ knowledge.
– Map the:
   a. Knowledge/content needed to achieve technical proficiency;
   b. What knowledge content you have to help people achieve technical proficiency;
   c. Location of the knowledge you have.
– Use this map (Figure 12, page 44) to identify gaps in technical knowledge, identify avenues for filling specific gaps, or finding expertise when needed.

5.   **The Expertise Tacit Knowledge Map**— The expertise tacit map is best used to identify specific experts and their areas of expertise. This typically works best inside a business unit or a division with similar units. We have used this map most often to identify the right people for after-action review or lesson learned sessions, or to highlight the appropriate people to participate in a particular community of practice. How?

– Identify the business function or business process that you will focus on.
– Develop or use existing process maps to begin knowledge mapping.
– Identify appropriate business management and experts to help you identify sources and owners of content/ knowledge.
– Map the content and knowledge sources and owners against the process map.
– Use this map (Figure 13, page 45) to identify appropriate experts for creating a company expertise location system, capturing lessons learned, performing after-action reviews, or validating tacit knowledge or information.

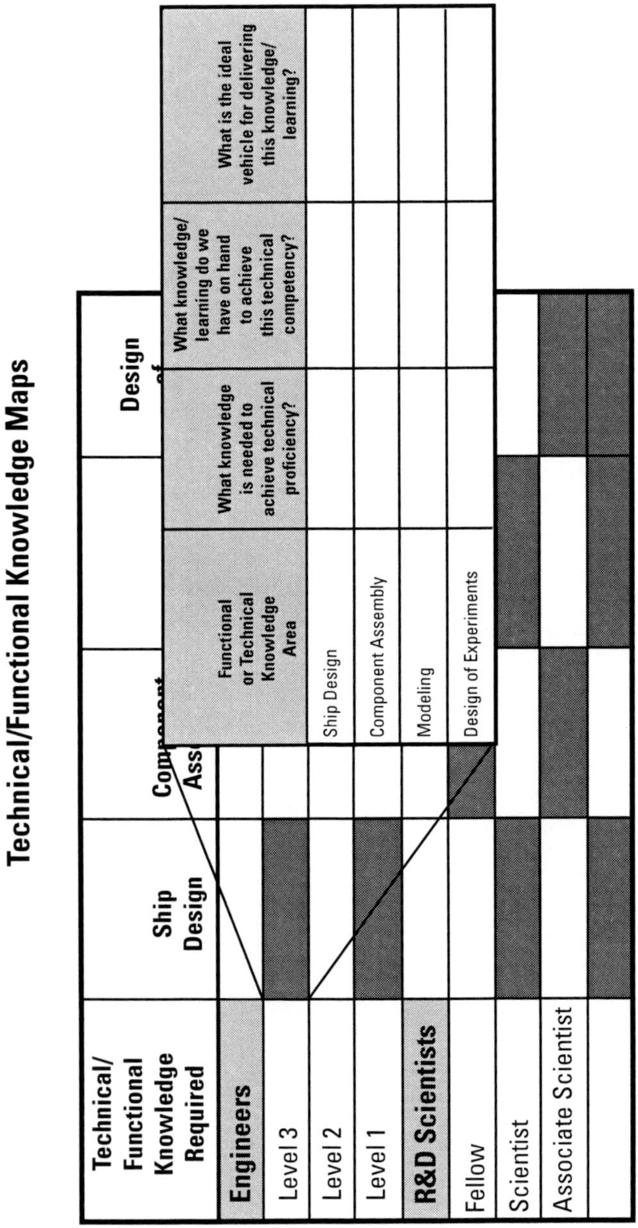

Technical/Functional Knowledge Maps

Technical/ Functional Knowledge Required	Ship Design	Component Assembly	Design of...	Functional or Technical Knowledge Area	What knowledge is needed to achieve technical proficiency?	What knowledge/ learning do we have on hand to achieve this technical competency?	What is the ideal vehicle for delivering this knowledge/ learning?
Engineers							
Level 3				Ship Design			
Level 2				Component Assembly			
Level 1				Modeling			
R&D Scientists				Design of Experiments			
Fellow							
Scientist							
Associate Scientist							

Figure 12

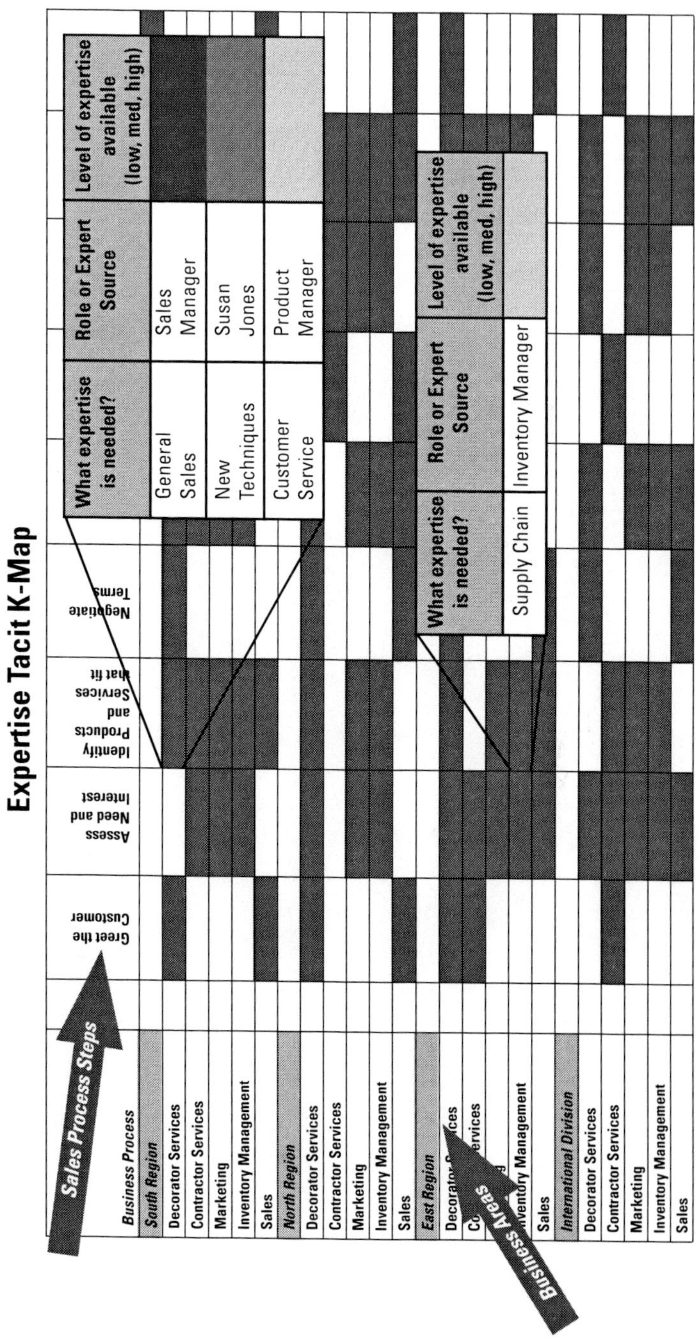

Expertise Tacit K-Map

Business Process	Greet the Customer	Assess Need and Interest	Identify Products and Services that fit	Negotiate Terms
South Region				
Decorator Services				
Contractor Services				
Marketing				
Inventory Management				
Sales				
North Region				
Decorator Services				
Contractor Services				
Marketing				
Inventory Management				
Sales				
East Region				
Decorator Services				
Contractor Services				
Inventory Management				
Sales				
International Division				
Decorator Services				
Contractor Services				
Marketing				
Inventory Management				
Sales				

What expertise is needed?	Role or Expert Source	Level of expertise available (low, med, high)
General Sales	Sales Manager	
New Techniques	Susan Jones	
Customer Service	Product Manager	

What expertise is needed?	Role or Expert Source	Level of expertise available (low, med, high)
Supply Chain	Inventory Manager	

Sales Process Steps

Business Areas

These are the people that should be included in the AAR process.

Figure 13

6. **The Document Explicit Knowledge Map** – To create specific knowledge management solutions, such as communities of practice, virtual collaboration tools, or best practice transfer processes, this is the baseline knowledge map we use to help identify specific knowledge assets, knowledge needs, and the sources, recipients, locations, and formats of that knowledge. How?
   - Develop or use existing process maps to begin knowledge mapping.
   - Identify appropriate business areas that impact the process
   - Pull together a design team that represents the business areas and processes being mapped.
   - Identify key knowledge to be mapped, sources, recipients, location of knowledge, tacit/explicit nature, routine/non-routine nature, and issues knowledge addresses.
   - Use this knowledge map (Figure 14) to create core content for a CoP, portal tool, or project team.

7. **The Job/Role-based Knowledge Map** – Some organizations need to explicitly map the knowledge needed for various job or roles to perform specific processes. This map, while similar to the functional/technical knowledge map, adds a layer of specificity. It identifies the specific knowledge managers think each job role needs to be successful. This map helps create an inventory of the knowledge assets (and what format they are in) for each role, ultimately helping to identify gaps and strengths. How?
   - Develop or use existing process maps to begin knowledge mapping;
   - Identify appropriate jobs/roles that engage in this process;
   - Pull together a design team that represents the job types and process being mapped;
   - Identify key knowledge to be mapped, sources, recipients, and location of knowledge;
   - Use this knowledge map (Figure 15, page 48) to identify learning/knowledge interventions needed to help each job successfully complete the process (to drive business results).

Document Explicit Tacit K-Map

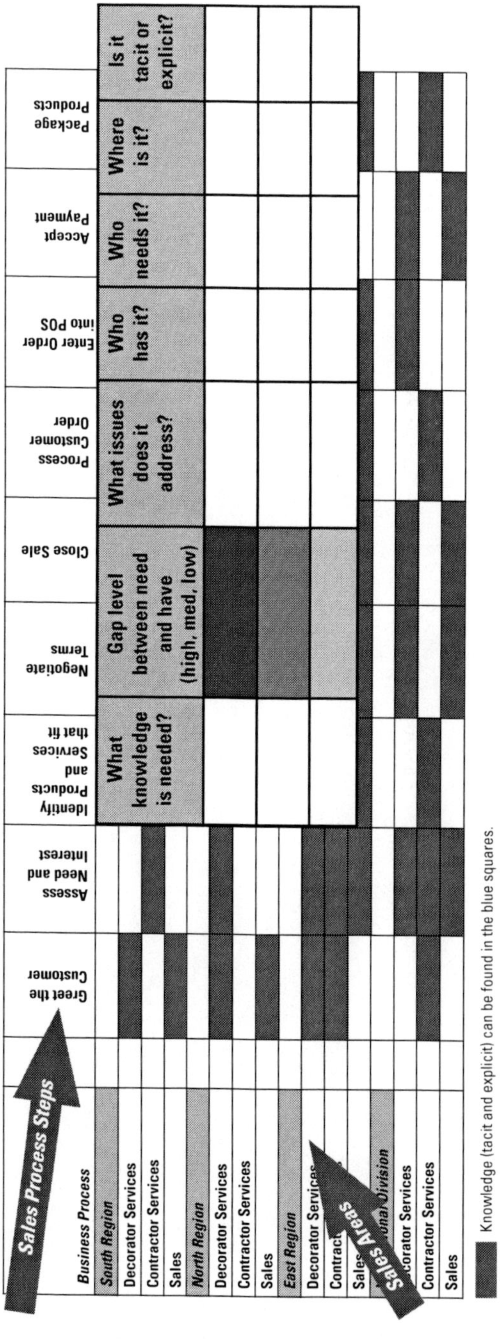

	Greet the Customer	Assess Need and Interest	Identify Products and Services that fit	Negotiate Terms	Close Sale	Process Customer Order	Enter Order into POS	Accept Payment	Package Products	Is it tacit or explicit?
Sales Process Steps / **Business Process**			What knowledge is needed?	Gap level between need and have (high, med, low)		What issues does it address?	Who has it?	Who needs it?	Where is it?	
South Region										
Decorator Services										
Contractor Services										
Sales										
North Region										
Decorator Services										
Contractor Services										
Sales										
East Region										
Decorator Services										
Contractor Services										
Sales										
Sales Areas / **Regional Division**										
Decorator Services										
Contractor Services										
Sales										

■ Knowledge (tacit and explicit) can be found in the blue squares.

Figure 14

Job/Role-based Knowledge Map

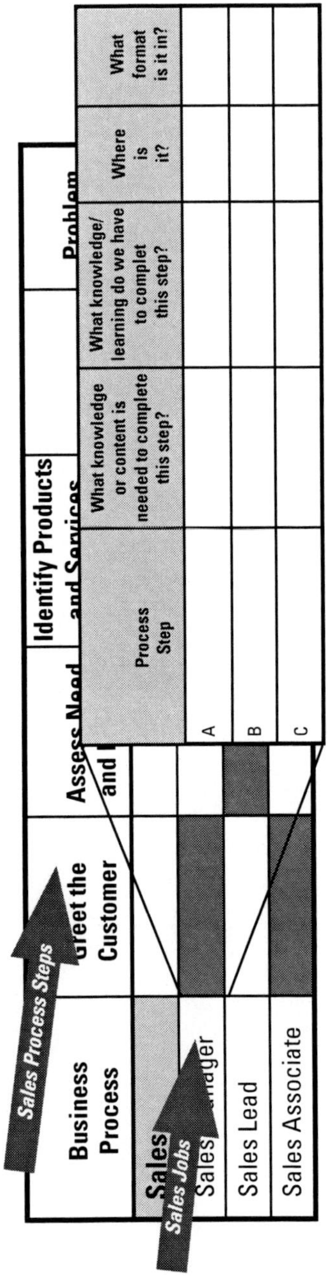

Figure 15

Gap Analysis

One of the most important steps when creating a knowledge map is to perform a gap analysis between what you found during the exercise and what you perceive to be the ideal state. This gap, or discrepancy of information, is the most specific, explicit information that can be extracted from a knowledge map. Gap analysis helps a knowledge mapping team prioritize and categorize process information, and also ensures that groups have the most valuable knowledge at their immediate disposal.

To perform a gap analysis, a knowledge management team should ask themselves the following questions:

- What critical knowledge is missing?
- What (or who) hinders the flow of knowledge within the process? Why?
- What (or who) enhances the flow of knowledge? Why?
- What are the next steps for the knowledge map? (What is it going to be used for?)

The next chapter will describe exactly how to create each one of these map types.

Chapter Four

Creating a Knowledge Map

Regardless of which template a you use, there are six basic steps to follow.

1. Select the process/focus area (scope of the map).
2. Clearly delineate and capture the key business reasons for mapping the knowledge (to ensure you will use it).
3. Map the processes and/or strategic goals of the organization.
   a. Identify key decision points and cross-functional hand-offs.
   b. Locate owners and stakeholders of highly-valued processes.
   c. Identify sources and recipients of knowledge.
4. Identify important knowledge assets needed for each step of the process or strategic goal.
   a. Create an inventory of types of knowledge used and needed (magnet content).
5. Identify gaps, lack of connectivity, and information overload.
6. Develop a plan for collecting, reviewing, validating, storing, and sharing the knowledge and information on your map.

An explanation of how to proceed through the steps using each type of knowledge map follows.

Strategic Overview Knowledge Map

Consider the situation at XYZ Corp. At an executive team meeting, a group finalized its strategic goals for the upcoming year. After two years of diminishing growth, the group decided that major shifts in focus would be needed. In the beginning of the year, managers were tasked: to focus on decreasing time-to-market for three key product segments; to deploy process improvement consistently throughout the organization; and to identify and penetrate new markets for their diverse set of technology products.

In Step 2, as these initiatives rolled to each business unit leader, it was clear that executing the strategy would require experience and expertise in order to: improve R&D cycle time; develop and deploy a hybrid Six Sigma/Lean process improvement program, and identify and close sales in new foreign markets.

In Step 3, the business unit heads of R&D, manufacturing, and development at XYZ Corp. separately approached the KM team leader to understand how they could identify, link, and deploy their knowledge assets to the new enterprise strategy. The KM lead recognized that knowledge mapping was the crucial first step in developing a coherent deployment strategy for each. The KM lead worked individually with each business unit head to identify key thought leaders to work on a strategic knowledge mapping task force. Starting with the strategic goals of the organization and of the individual business unit components, the teams mapped out the key processes that enabled that strategy to be realized.

During Step 4, the task force interviewed key employees, thought leaders, and managers to uncover the knowledge and/or competencies they needed to improve the process areas for the strategic goal area. After prioritizing these answers into simple categories of importance, they asked these same individuals what knowledge/competencies they actually had on hand in those areas.

The group at XYZ Corp. then performed a gap analysis in Step 5 between the desired knowledge/competency areas and the current knowledge/competency available to each organization. The group then documented how the current knowledge/competencies could be accessed as a first step towards connecting needed knowledge assets (both people and content) with the business processes that required them.

At the end of XYZ Corp.'s exercise, in Step 6, the task forces created recommendations for filling the knowledge/competency gaps – in some cases this was hiring new experts, engaging consultants and/or contractors for training and capability building. In others, it created cross-business communities of practice and an expertise location system to connect the organization.

The Expertise Overview Knowledge Map

The president of a medium-sized, global oil and gas services company engaged a strategy consulting firm to develop a five-year strategy for the organization to identify and exploit market development opportunities for continued growth. One of these recommendations was for the organization to begin using integrated project teams for jobs that required the resources of more than one business unit. In the past, the organization confused clients by having different points of contact, communication vehicles, sales tools, and messages from each business unit that worked on a particular job. A streamlined and integrated project team, led by an experienced project manager with a cross-functional background, was critical to leveraging the knowledge of the organization and providing true and lasting value to current and potential clients.

This strategy could ultimately serve as a competitive advantage in the industry. However, the president realized that he had a demographic problem – his small cadre of experienced project managers could serve in this capacity today, but many were within two years of retirement age. After that, the experience base of the organization was varied and widely unknown. How could he push this effort without an understanding of the expertise available to him?

In Step 2 of the oil and gas service company's efforts, the president approached the KM team lead to help him map the expertise within the organization. In Step 3, The KM team leader approached the senior leaders of each function that would be part of the integrated project effort so that he/she could understand the various locations and business processes that each was engaged in. After prioritizing the areas of expertise needed to work in the integrated project approach, the HR manager from each unit was interviewed to ascertain levels of expertise and age of the workforce. The team pulled information from the competency database and evaluations from the previous year to identify likely candidates.

In Step 4, the HR manager put together a map for the president that noted the expertise categories needed, the overall experience level available (based on years of service and percentage of certified project managers) and the risk level of losing that expertise (low, medium, and high with corresponding characteristics of each).

The company then proceeded to Step 5. At the presentation to the president, the KM team lead noted that while there was a high risk of losing high level project expertise, there was a small cadre of medium-term employees (12-15 years) in the European region that had many of the skills that would translate to success. Upon investigation, the president found that this cadre had sufficient technical and project management skills but still rated low on leadership training and presentation skills.

In Step 6, the HR manager and KM team lead devised a combined training and knowledge sharing plan that included on-line and classroom training as well as a community of practice with the older, experienced project managers. In 12 months, this group was ready to begin assuming these new roles.

The Competency and Learning Needs Knowledge Map

While setting the strategic direction of his R&D unit for the next two years, the senior vice president of R&D at a diversified aerospace/defense contractor realized that he did not have a good handle on either the current competencies of his employee base, or the learning/competency needs that his new strategy would require.

To solve this problem, he initiated a knowledge mapping process.

In Step 2, he enlisted his organization's KM and HR development teams to develop a competency and learning needs knowledge map for the various types of scientists and engineers employed in R&D against the competencies he felt were vital to long term success.

In Step 3, the team first mapped out the various levels of R&D scientists and engineers (associate scientist, fellow, level 1 engineer, etc.). Next, the team used the senior vice president's list of goals for the next three years and created a list of the most important competencies required to meet those goals. These included things such as building partnerships, decision-making, financial management, planning, and problem solving. Because the competencies for each grade did not exist, the team created descriptions of each competency for each major job grade.

Next, the group took each job area and mapped it against each competency. They asked "What knowledge or learning is needed to fulfill each competency for each skill area?" The group investigated what knowledge and/or learning resources were currently available in the form of best practices, communities of practice, learning modules, or training courses to achieve that level of proficiency.

In Step 5, after discussing gaps in the functional knowledge and learning offerings with the senior vice president, the team was able to develop a tool that allowed individual employees to assess their skills, using their current performance plan, against the noted criteria for their role and the roles above them.

Finally, the group identified the ideal vehicle for delivering the knowledge/learning for each group – in some cases this was on the job training, in others it was participation in a community of practice. The KM and HR team also implemented a learning management system that would allow the organization to "push" knowledge and learning objects to each individual around their skill gaps. Finally, the team created a tool to allow the senior vice president (and other officers) the ability to see roll-up reports of the competency levels for each of the employee categories. This enabled the senior vice president to draw up resourcing, training budgets, and business plans that made sense.

The Technical/Functional Knowledge Maps

The technical/functional knowledge maps are very similar to the learning/competency maps; however the former looks at specific technical or functional knowledge (e.g., ship design, component assembly, etc.), while the latter looks at competency areas (e.g. planning, problem solving, decision making). Both can be used to inform senior management about the current state of expertise in critical technical disciplines or key business competency areas. Together, they can offer a clear picture of what senior managers need to do to bolster their skill sets and ultimately achieve their goals.

The Expertise Tacit Knowledge Map

A large regional utility in the southwestern United States, in the process of deregulation, was required to improve its service restoration process to meet Public Utility Commission mandates for customer outage minutes. Because the organization's services zones covered a densely populated and geographically dispersed area, large storms often required resources to be marshaled from regions 50 to 60 miles from the epicenter of the storm. Depending on the size and severity of the storm, hundreds or thousands of workers could be called upon at any time to coordinate manpower, fix circuits and breakers, report on status, and move equipment. The utility company formed a special team to look at ways to continuously improve this process; unfortunately, these "lessons learned" meetings were attended by dozens of people and often degraded into blame sessions in which each group accused others for delays and missed targets.

In Step 2, the leader of the team, noting that PUC targets had to be reached regardless of who was to blame, realized that a more structured approach would be necessary for the team to understand root causes of issues, develop improvement recommendations, and foster buy-in from all of the concerned groups. He pulled together a sub team to explore options and decided to create an after-action review process, modeled on the U.S. Army's version, to identify and manage the improvement process. He asked an outside expert in knowledge management and after-action review to help set up the process.

In Step 3, the consultant and the service restoration team mapped the eight main process steps of service restoration, from identifying storm possibilities to returning crews to home service areas. After mapping the process, the group asked what type of expertise was needed during each specific step of the service restoration process. This included things like dispatching, work crew knowledge, district support, and weather reporting. In Step 4, the team noted where that expertise existed in each district – in some cases it was a single individual, in others it was based on a specific role. In Step 5, the team rated the levels of expertise of those individuals using tenure and the number of storm events conducted and identified significant gap areas. Finally, in Step 6, the team was able to use this knowledge map to develop an invitation list for each after-action review that pulled in only the appropriate representatives from each process step, region, and group. This allowed the group to target the after-action review on just the groups that participated, and after setting ground rules for discussion, resulted in crisp two-hour meetings with high member satisfaction. As a result, the service restoration realized a 20 percent improvement in reliability in the first year and was able to more effectively target its process improvement efforts.

The Document Explicit Knowledge Map

The new senior vice president of the transportation practice in a large engineering company found that her teams were spending more and more time and effort working with community groups on large projects. In a recent case, the towns along a major highway corridor leading to several popular ski resorts were bogged down with terrible traffic but would not get any tax benefit from widening the corridor, which the engineering company had been tasked to do. However, the ski resorts needed the corridor widened to promote and increase the traffic they needed to continue growing.

Counties formed groups against the widening and held up projects for years as they looked for concessions. Luckily, the senior vice president was an experienced public strategy consultant and helped form a team to address the issues, come up with several billion dollars for improvements, and successfully negotiate a satisfactory conclusion. She depended heavily on her own tacit knowledge and that of the small group of like-minded professionals in the firm to create numerous public workshops and other new tools that helped bring about consensus. In her new role, however, she noticed that projects across the country were running into similar snags and that most project managers were not equipped to handle the public relations, negotiation, and consensus building tasks that were necessary for success.

In Step 1, she tasked one of her public involvement specialists to create a community of practice around public involvement in hopes of improving the organization's capacity to respond to public issues while improving the skill sets of those that worked in this field.

In Step 2, the team worked with a KM specialist to assist with the creation of the community – the first step of which was to perform a document explicit knowledge map. In Step 3, a small sub team of seven public involvement practitioners began by mapping out the typical process they used to engage and assist project managers with public strategies. Next, the team identified what knowledge or content was needed by the practitioners at each step of the process. Using the template below, the group then noted what knowledge or content they could currently access for each of those process steps.

In Step 4, the group identified the sources of that knowledge/content (in some cases it was an individual, in others a handbook or database), who typically needed that knowledge/content (they found, in a few instances, that no one needed it and so they realized that that knowledge was no longer important to capture), where that knowledge/content was located, and the format that it was in (electronic, in someone's head, etc.). In Step 5, the team performed a gap analysis between current and desired knowledge assets and created a goal for the community of practice to fill the noted gaps. Because the group's goal was to quickly connect the public involvement practitioners to the other experts in the field and to the most high value codified templates and knowledge, in Step 6 the group was able to use the knowledge map to mine each other's repositories and build a Web-based knowledge repository and roster of members. After six months, the group measured its results and found that they spent 45 percent less time looking for best practices on public involvement and 25 percent less time answering public involvement questions because they could direct project managers to the body of knowledge. The commensurate improvements in satisfaction with their clients (both the internal project managers and the external customers) resulted in more billable work for the public involvement practitioners and higher revenues for the organization.

The Job/Role—Based Knowledge Map

The director of sales at a large, growing retail store realized that his training costs were spiraling out of control. In his high-turnover establishment, he was having to spend more time training employees on ever-more sophisticated products and then watched them walk out the door for other jobs, school, or to competitors. Because the organization had not documented the specific types and categories of knowledge needed by sales people in various roles, the training and learning program was notoriously inconsistent.

Some store managers followed a dedicated process that taught the sales process, product knowledge, customer service skills, and decision making. Others covered basic product knowledge and handed employees a book. Customers complained that sales people were not able to answer their questions, and sales people were frustrated because they were not able to tap into the knowledge of the organization. In Step 2, the director of sales asked a group of his best sales reps and a store manager to create a job/role-based learning program to improve the training program while simultaneously improving customer satisfaction and retention rates.

In Step 3, the group started by process mapping the typical sales process. Next, they identified each job that supported or performed that process. In Step 4, they looked at the knowledge or content needed by each job to complete each step, identified which of those knowledge/content assets they currently had within the company, identified the location and the format it was in. In Step 5, they used the Learning/Competency map to identify the level of competency needed to be proficient at each process step and the ideal vehicle for delivering the knowledge/content to employees. Finally, in Step 6, the team recommended a blended training model for each job/role that mixed classroom, online-learning, on the job coaching, and a community of practice in their sales area. The sales director implemented the program in one region and discovered that his employee satisfaction ratings went up by 25 percent, retention improved 20 percent, and customer satisfaction with salespeople's knowledge improved by 35 percent.

Chapter Five

Helpful Tools
for Creating a Knowledge Map

Knowledge maps can be as sophisticated or as simple as you need them to be. For most, a process map, flip chart, sticky notes, the right people, and Microsoft Excel are all a knowledge mapping team needs to create an effective map. A few additional resources follow that a knowledge mapping team may use to facilitate the process.

Tools

The most important tools for effective knowledge mapping are the right people (who understand the processes or knowledge domains being mapped, process maps, and pen and paper. Mind Mapping software, Microsoft Word, Excel, PowerPoint, Visio, and many other common desktop publishing or graphical tools can be used for knowledge mapping. The key is to create a set of templates that allow you to quickly and easily map the knowledge and content against known functions or processes for easy manipulation, planning, and classification.

Social Network Analysis (SNA)

One of the hottest knowledge management tools on the market is the Social Network Analysis (SNA) tool, championed by many practitioners with various spins on the tool and analysis methods. Social Network Analysis is the mapping and measuring of relationships and flows between people, groups, organizations, computers or other information/knowledge processing entities. The nodes in the network are the people and groups while the links show relationships or flows between the nodes. SNA provides both a visual and a mathematical analysis of human relationships. Management consultants use this methodology with their business clients and call it Organizational Network Analysis (ONA).

The purpose of SNAs are similar to other knowledge maps—to help you find and understand the knowledge brokers in your organization and where gaps in connectivity exist. Knowledge brokers are those individuals in the organization who tend to have more contacts in their network overall and more contacts outside their department and organization. They are more likely to be sought out for information, are more aware of information sources in the network, have more new people in their networks, and invest more time and effort in their networks.[5] Below is a simplified depiction of a social network analysis (Figure 17)—for more information, please visit http://www.ickn.org/.

Knowledge Mapping Checklist:
- Begin with the end in mind by clearly stating the goal of the knowledge mapping exercise. What are you going to do with it that will impact business performance?
- Gather any strategy documents, goal statements, process maps, and competency maps needed before beginning.
- Collect appropriate organization charts.
- Assemble any previously created catalogs or repositories of standard operating procedures, databases, and knowledge sources.
- Ensure you have a sufficient supply of butcher paper, note paper, permanent markers, and tape.
- Recruit someone with a laptop and working knowledge of MS Excel, Visio, PowerPoint, and Word.

---

[5] Gloor, Peter, pgloor@mit.edu.

Social Network Analysis

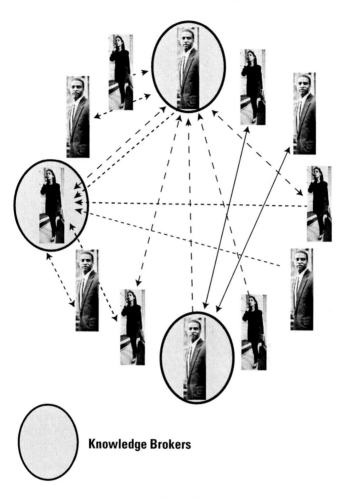

Knowledge Brokers

Figure 17

- Identify and recruit the appropriate members for your team, keeping in mind the following elements:

  1. Name a facilitator who can assist in setting up and managing the process of knowledge mapping.

  2. Choose a content editor who serves as the point person for collecting content and creating and distributing the knowledge map(s).

  3. Appoint a group of validators with subject matter expertise who can fill in gaps, authenticate results, and point to important related sources of knowledge and identify competitive intelligence resources for any current repositories they manage.

  4. Tap into HR resources for any expertise, competency, or learning assets.

  5. Bring appropriate business management in to shape and scope the effort.

  6. Utilize corporate librarians or data specialists if possible.

  7. Keep the team to 5-10 people for manageable work processes, but don't be afraid to consult others as needed.

  8. Ensure that process owners and operators are represented.

     - Scope the level of inquiry: Are you looking at knowledge found in discussion threads, conversations, documentation, communities of practice, "official" intellectual assets, customers and/or suppliers?

     - Develop an action plan for gathering the knowledge and content.

     - Typical roles include facilitator (who understands process mapping tools), content gatherer, process owner, and classification specialist.

     - Use the templates and questions in chapter 4 to knowledge map.

     - Execute your action plan and conduct the gap analysis to help determine where changes need to happen.

     - Use your knowledge map to make changes to process, functions, tools, or learning in your organization.

LESSONS LEARNED IN KNOWLEDGE MAPPING

- Begin with the end business goal in mind. If you are mapping for the sake of mapping, you've lost. What will a knowledge map help you to do more efficiently, with higher quality, or with lower costs?

- Keep the 80/20 Rule in Mind--The 80/20 rule applies to knowledge mapping just as it does to many other improvement tools: 20 percent of the information will provide 80 percent of the value. In other words, map the most important and frequently used knowledge first. It should be used as a springboard when initiating a knowledge mapping process.

- High level mapping of the process you want to share knowledge around is key! Without the language of the business process to inform and enlighten, knowledge exists without context.

- Recruit the right people-- Extracting information from people's heads that are easily accessible will give you 20 percent of the information, but 80 percent of the value. The challenge is filling the map out as soon as possible by engaging others on the team.

- Accurately collect and update knowledge maps. All knowledge maps become outdated and need to be reviewed at least yearly. Some industries, such as the high-tech industry, may require updates every six months.

As you can see, mapping an organization's knowledge assets can lead to stronger management, more efficient processes, and better collaboration. As we began this journey, we called the reader's attention to the simple and familiar analogy of using a road map to plan a vacation. As we moved through a discussion of knowledge, knowledge management, and the knowledge flow process, we hope you were able to ground yourself in the thinking that has made knowledge mapping such a vital part of good business today. In Chapters three and four, we outlined several types and styles of knowledge maps that might be useful in your organization. Again, we have found that different situations call for different types of questions, focus, and outputs – hopefully these choices will provide ample options for your particular need. Finally, we included several checklists and assessments to help you structure the exercise and keep your knowledge maps current.

The journey just begins as you finish your knowledge mapping exercises – making positive impacts on your organization, improving its job training, realigning its key expertise, and connecting relevant work groups. In all cases, remember to apply the appropriate amount of effort and specificity for the job at hand—neither too much, nor too little for the outcome you expect. Finally, keep the business of the business in mind as you map and link your knowledge assets together . Without that singular focus, your results can quickly become irrelevant, but with it, you can improve your enterprise and drive it to the desired destination.

Glossary of Terms

Knowledge Management

Absorptive Capacity

The ability of a group to recognize the value of new, external information, assimilate it, and apply it to commercial ends is largely a function of the group's level of prior related knowledge that could include:

- basic skills,
- shared language,
- knowledge of recent scientific or industry developments,
- technology, and
- culture.

Acquired Knowledge

A source of knowledge in which the knowledge comes from outside of the organization—The knowledge can be purchased or "rented."

Adaptation

Knowledge that results from responding to new processes or technologies in the market place—If organizations do not adapt, they will cease to remain competitive.

Advisory Board

A cross-functional advisory team that represents respected thought leaders throughout the organization, typically made up of vice president and director-level people—The purpose of the advisory board is to:

- provide a forum for surfacing, addressing, and solving shared KM issues and needs;
- create, capture, and leverage KM best practices and approaches;

- support communities of practice and collaboration methods for transfer of high-value tacit knowledge;
- communicate KM messages and successes (internally and externally); and
- advocate and support common processes for knowledge access, management, and use.

Aggregator

An organization that combines information such as news, sports scores, weather forecasts, and reference materials from various sources and makes it available to its customers (source TechWeb Technology Encyclopedia)

Assessment Tools

A listing of criteria and guidelines for using criteria to evaluate a given situation—The guidelines might be a scoring or priority system.

Best Practices

An assessment recommending the most appropriate way of handling a certain type of task, based on an observation of the way that several organizations handle that task.

Best-practice Community of Practice

Best-practice communities focus on developing, validating, and disseminating specific practices. Best-practice communities ask members to continuously develop and implement practices.

Blueprints

A means of recording detailed design plans for a knowledge management system—Blueprints provide a road map through the content (like a floor plan in a blueprint for a building), screen-by-screen plans for preparing the content (like the elevations), technical specifications for building the software, templates for preparing content that must follow a specific format (such as entries into a lessons learned database), approved terminology lists, and other editorial guidelines (like the specifications in a blueprint for a building).

Client Computers

Individual computers in clients' offices—These are generally the computers that the average person uses.

Collaborative Enterprise Management

Collaborative Enterprise Management (CEM) combines the focus associated with performance management, the power of structured collaboration and business intelligence, and a scalable supporting technology. CEM combines the collective results of individuals with the power of alignment that comes from working together toward a shared objective.

Communities of Practice (CoP)

Networks of people, small and large, who come together to share and to learn from one another face-to-face and virtually—These communities – of practice, of interest, of learning – are held together by a common goal and purpose that is supported by a desire to share experiences, insights, and best practices.

Content Management

Software that helps developers track the location of information (especially important in medium and large systems, where the location of content can be easily forgotten) and relationships among the different pieces of information.

Data

Facts and figures presented out of context for the purpose of innovation or improved efficiency.

Database

A collection of related information, which is structured for easy access to specific pieces of information.

Data Mining

A process of reviewing information in a database and making new connections among the information.

Dedicated Resources

Knowledge that results from an organization setting aside some staff members or an entire department (usually research and development) to develop new intellectual property.

Design Team

A cross-functional team that represents the business unit or functional area of a KM initiative—Typically, this group includes both management and line representation. The purpose of the advisory board is to:

- refine the scope of the pilots or initiatives;
- identify the pilot users and "high-voltage knowledge" to achieve early success;
- analyze costs and the infrastructure required;
- recommend communication, training, rewards, and other issues affecting cultural acceptance of a KM approach; and
- plan projects with staged activities and milestones.

Explicit Knowledge

Knowledge that can be written down or expressed verbally.

Firewall

Software that "separates" information so it is only available to users within an organization, not to all users of the World Wide Web—In some instances, the software prompts users to enter an identifying name and password to indicate that they have authority to gain access to the network.

Fusion

Knowledge created by bringing together people with different perspectives to work on the same project.

Helping Community of Practice

These communities focus on connecting members so they can ask for help on specific problems, learn the areas of expertise of other community members, and get to know each other well enough to understand each others perspective. By informally discussing their individual practices and technical problems, they build enough trust to truly admit problems and share ideas they are still formulating.

Human Capital

The knowledge-power that comes and goes from an organization each day—This is another way of describing the knowledge that resides in the heads of employees and that has not been shared with others.

Index

(1) A list (as of bibliographical information or citations to a body of literature) arranged usually in alphabetical order of some specified datum (as author, subject, or keyword). (2) A list of items (as topics or names) treated in a printed work that gives for each item the page number where it may be found. (source: Merriam-Webster dictionary)

Information

Data that is presented in context, so people might make use of it.

Innovation Community of Practice

These communities help members cross boundaries to generate new ideas.

Innovation

Any new idea, method, or device developed by an individual, group, or organization.

Intellectual Capital

An effort by organizations to place a financial value on its tacit and explicit knowledge.

Intelligent Agents

Software that works without the assistance of users by making choices—The choices are based on rules of behavior that software developers have identified and built into the software.

Interface

A linkage, usually between a computer and a user, or among computer programs—An interface between a computer and user refers to the elements of the computer and software that the user interacts with: the screens, icons, menus, and dialogues. An interface among computer programs involves using agreed-upon commands and statements that let one computer program exchange information with the other in a way that the first program can integrate the second program.

Knowledge

Information in action; information that people make use of, along with the rules and contexts of its use.

Knowledge Assets

Intellectual properties that generate a cash flow for the organization. Examples include patents, copyrighted material, and licenses.

Knowledge Base

A central database of information about a particular topic or organization—An infobase typically includes information from all parts of an organization.

Knowledge Hoarding

The practice of limiting the flow of information either by controlling its flow or failing to share it.

Knowledge Management

Systematic approaches to help information and knowledge flow to the right people at the right time so they can act more efficiently and effectively to find, understand, share, and use knowledge to create value.

Knowledge Networking

Knowledge resulting from people sharing information with one another formally or informally: Knowledge networking often occurs within disciplines (such as programmers communicating with one another) and projects (such as all of the people working on a new software product sharing information with one another).

Knowledge Stewarding Community of Practice

These communities see their role as organizing, managing, and retaining the collective knowledge of the community, including the materials their members use day-to-day.

Lessons Learned

A reflection on the knowledge that someone should take with them from this experience into similar ones—These lessons often reflect on "what we did right," "what we would do differently," and "how we could improve our process and product to be more effective in the future."

Mass Customization

A basic product that is available in a variety of forms, each tailored for a different audience (such as new or experienced users) or need (such as training or marketing)—The audience perceives that the information was customized just for them, but the developers of that information do not have to write separate versions of the information for each audience.

Meta-tagging

Classification data that is stored on the computer with the information—Users facilitate the retrieval of it by using agreed-upon terminology as well as formats that software can easily scan.

Metcalf's Law

"Power is a function of the square of the size of the network."

Moore's Law

The phenomenon that the capacity of the microprocessors that form the nucleus of a computer doubles approximately every 18 months—Similar improvements to telecommunications capacity occur approximately every five months.

Non-competitors

Organizations that do not seek the same business or clients that you do but from whom you might glean best practices and lessons learned—Although neither the best practices nor lessons learned might appear to be relevant at first glance, on the surface, they can be shown to transfer to your industry.

Object-Oriented Programming

A method of preparing parts of computer applications in which programmers develop a series of small programs, each of which performs a discrete task—These modules can be used repeatedly by a variety of programs. To create a software application or program, programmers link these generic modules together. This same approach underlies the mass-customization of information.

Portal
> Special Web pages that organize access to all of the online resources about a topic, providing a one-stop shop of sorts—A portal acts as a gateway to information sources and analysis tools for decision makers at appropriate places in an organization. Portals give real-time, single-point-of-access to the wealth of information and tools located both inside and outside the organization. Portals may present information from a broad array of sources such as project databases, data warehouses, and ERP systems, reports, presentations, emails, and external content providers. Portals may also support collaboration by giving users access to collaboration tools that link corporate experts and industry communities.

Profiles or Profiling Software
> Programs that assist organizations in describing users with minimal direct involvement of those users; these descriptions are called profiles.

Server Computers
> Central computers that most users within the organization have access to. Organizations typically store commonly used data and programs on servers, such as price lists, employee directories, and training courses.

Single Sourcing
> The act of displaying online or printing information from the same file (called the source).

Single-Sourcing Tools
> Software that lets developers prepare a single source file of data and display it in a number of ways online and in print. Adobe's Portable Document Format (PDF) is one such tool.

Steering Committee
> A cross-functional team that represents respected thought leaders throughout the organization, typically made up the highest-level officers of the organization. The purpose of the steering committee is to: provide funding, run interference, sign off on KM initiatives, and promote knowledge sharing throughout the enterprise.

Structural Capital
> The power-wielding knowledge that remains when employees leave.

Tacit Knowledge

Knowledge that resides in the minds of individuals and is surfaced in response to a situation or action.

Taxonomy

The study of the general principles of the science of classification; especially the orderly classification of plants and animals according to their presumed natural relationships. (Merriam-Webster Dictionary)

The ease and speed with which people can find information, and the accuracy of their interpretation and application of that information.

XML, Extended Markup Language

A successor technology to the markup language HTML that lets developers prepare information as small chunks that can be mixed and matched at the time it is displayed online.

Yellow Pages

Like the phone directory that lists organizations by the type of service they provide, the yellow pages is an online directory that lists individuals and departments by the expertise and services they provide. Large organizations in which people typically are not aware of the full breadth of expertise inside the company find these yellow pages extremely helpful.